I0494216

INAPPROPRIATE CRITERIA WERE USED TO IDENTIFY TAX-EXEMPT APPLICATIONS FOR REVIEW

Highlights

Final Report issued on May 14, 2013

Highlights of Reference Number: 2013-10-053 to the Internal Revenue Service Acting Commissioner, Tax Exempt and Government Entities Division.

IMPACT ON TAXPAYERS

Early in Calendar Year 2010, the IRS began using inappropriate criteria to identify organizations applying for tax-exempt status to review for indications of significant political campaign intervention. Although the IRS has taken some action, it will need to do more so that the public has reasonable assurance that applications are processed without unreasonable delay in a fair and impartial manner in the future.

WHY TIGTA DID THE AUDIT

TIGTA initiated this audit based on concerns expressed by members of Congress. The overall objective of this audit was to determine whether allegations were founded that the IRS: 1) targeted specific groups applying for tax-exempt status, 2) delayed processing of targeted groups' applications, and 3) requested unnecessary information from targeted groups.

WHAT TIGTA FOUND

The IRS used inappropriate criteria that identified for review Tea Party and other organizations applying for tax-exempt status based upon their names or policy positions instead of indications of potential political campaign intervention. Ineffective management: 1) allowed inappropriate criteria to be developed and stay in place for more than 18 months, 2) resulted in substantial delays in processing certain applications, and 3) allowed unnecessary information requests to be issued.

Although the processing of some applications with potential significant political campaign

intervention was started soon after receipt, no work was completed on the majority of these applications for 13 months. This was due to delays in receiving assistance from the Exempt Organizations function Headquarters office. For the 296 total political campaign intervention applications TIGTA reviewed as of December 17, 2012, 108 had been approved, 28 were withdrawn by the applicant, none had been denied, and 160 were open from 206 to 1,138 calendar days (some for more than three years and crossing two election cycles).

More than 20 months after the initial case was identified, processing the cases began in earnest. Many organizations received requests for additional information from the IRS that included unnecessary, burdensome questions (e.g., lists of past and future donors). The IRS later informed some organizations that they did not need to provide previously requested information. IRS officials stated that any donor information received in response to a request from its Determinations Unit was later destroyed.

WHAT TIGTA RECOMMENDED

TIGTA recommended that the IRS finalize the interim actions taken, better document the reasons why applications potentially involving political campaign intervention are chosen for review, develop a process to track requests for assistance, finalize and publish guidance, develop and provide training to employees before each election cycle, expeditiously resolve remaining political campaign intervention cases (some of which have been in process for three years), and request that social welfare activity guidance be developed by the Department of the Treasury.

In their response to the report, IRS officials agreed with seven of our nine recommendations and proposed alternative corrective actions for two of our recommendations. TIGTA does not agree that the alternative corrective actions will accomplish the intent of the recommendations and continues to believe that the IRS should better document the reasons why applications potentially involving political campaign intervention are chosen for review and finalize and publish guidance.

DEPARTMENT OF THE TREASURY

WASHINGTON, D.C. 20220

TREASURY INSPECTOR GENERAL
FOR TAX ADMINISTRATION

May 14, 2013

MEMORANDUM FOR ACTING COMMISSIONER, TAX EXEMPT AND GOVERNMENT ENTITIES DIVISION

[signature]

FROM: Michael E. McKenney
                          Acting Deputy Inspector General for Audit

SUBJECT: Final Audit Report – Inappropriate Criteria Were Used to Identify
                          Tax-Exempt Applications for Review (Audit # 201210022)

This report presents the results of our review to determine whether allegations were founded that the Internal Revenue Service (IRS): 1) targeted specific groups applying for tax-exempt status, 2) delayed processing of targeted groups' applications for tax-exempt status, and 3) requested unnecessary information from targeted groups. This audit was initiated based on concerns expressed by members of Congress and reported in the media regarding the IRS's treatment of organizations applying for tax-exempt status. This review is included in our Fiscal Year 2013 Annual Audit Plan and addresses the major management challenge of Tax Compliance Initiatives.

We would like to clarify a few issues based on the IRS response to our report. The response states that our report views approvals as evidence that the Exempt Organizations function should not have looked closely at those applications. We disagree with this statement. Our objection was to the criteria used to identify these applications for review. We believe all applications should be reviewed prior to approval to determine whether tax-exempt status should be granted. The IRS's response also states that issues discussed in the report have been resolved. We disagree with this statement as well. Nine recommendations were made to correct concerns we raised in the report, and corrective actions have not been fully implemented. Further, as our report notes, a substantial number of applications have been under review, some for more than three years and through two election cycles, and remain open. Until these cases are closed by the IRS and our recommendations are fully implemented, we do not consider the concerns in this report to be resolved. Management's complete response to the draft report is included as Appendix VIII.

Copies of this report are also being sent to the IRS managers affected by the report recommendations. If you have any questions, please contact me or Gregory D. Kutz, Assistant Inspector General for Audit (Management Services and Exempt Organizations).

Table of Contents

Abbreviations

BOLO	Be On the Look Out
EO	Exempt Organizations
I.R.C.	Internal Revenue Code
IRS	Internal Revenue Service

Background

Organizations, such as charities, seeking Federal tax exemption are required to file an application with the Internal Revenue Service (IRS). Other organizations, such as social welfare organizations, may file an application but are not required to do so. The IRS's Exempt Organizations (EO) function, Rulings and Agreements office, which is headquartered in Washington, D.C., is responsible for processing applications for tax exemption. Within the Rulings and Agreements office, the Determinations Unit in Cincinnati, Ohio, is responsible for reviewing applications as they are received to determine whether the organization qualifies for tax-exempt status.

In Fiscal Year 2012,[1] 70 percent of all closed applications for tax-exempt status were approved during an initial review with little or no additional information from the organizations. If substantial additional information is needed, the application is placed in unassigned inventory until it can be assigned to a specialist in the Determinations Unit for further processing. The specialist develops a letter(s) requesting the additional information and issues it to the organization. Once the specialist receives all the necessary information to determine whether an organization should be afforded tax-exempt status, a final determination letter is issued to the organization either approving or denying the request for tax-exempt status.

If the Determinations Unit needs technical assistance processing applications, it may call upon the Technical Unit in the Rulings and Agreements office in Washington, D.C.[2] The IRS's goal for processing all types of applications for tax-exempt status was 121 days in Fiscal Year 2012; however, some cases may take substantially longer. For example, the EO function states in its *Fiscal Year 2013 Work Plan* that applications requiring additional information are not assigned for review until an average of five months after they are received.

Most organizations requesting tax-exempt status must submit either a Form 1023, *Application for Recognition of Exemption Under Section 501(c)(3) of the Internal Revenue Code*, or Form 1024, *Application for Recognition of Exemption Under Section 501(a)*, depending on the type of tax-exempt organization it desires to be. For example, a charitable organization would request exemption under Internal Revenue Code (I.R.C.) Section (§) 501(c)(3),[3] whereas a social welfare organization would request exemption under I.R.C. § 501(c)(4).[4]

---

[1] A 12-consecutive-month period ending on the last day of any month. The Federal Government's fiscal year begins on October 1 and ends on September 30.
[2] For a high-level organizational chart of offices referenced in this report, see Appendix V.
[3] I.R.C. § 501(c)(3) (2012).
[4] I.R.C. § 501(c)(4) (2012).

The I.R.C. section and subsection an organization is granted tax exemption under affects the activities it may undertake. For example, I.R.C. § 501(c)(3) charitable organizations are prohibited from directly or indirectly participating in or intervening in any political campaign on behalf of or in opposition to any candidate for public office (hereafter referred to as political campaign intervention).[5] However, I.R.C. § 501(c)(4) social welfare organizations, I.R.C. § 501(c)(5)[6] agricultural and labor organizations, and I.R.C. § 501(c)(6)[7] business leagues may engage in limited political campaign intervention. Figure 1 highlights certain characteristics of common types of tax-exempt organizations.

Figure 1: Characteristics of Certain Common Types of Tax-Exempt Organizations

Characteristic	I.R.C. § 501(c)(3)	I.R.C. §§ 501(c)(4), (c)(5), and (c)(6)
May receive tax deductible charitable contributions.	Yes	No
May engage in political campaign intervention.	No	Limited (must not constitute primary activity of organization)
Must publicly disclose the identity of its donors.	No	No
May engage in lobbying[8] (*i.e.*, legislative activity).	Limited (must not be substantial)	Yes (unlimited amount if in furtherance of tax-exempt purposes)
May engage in general advocacy[9] not related to legislation or the election of candidates.	Yes (permitted as an educational activity)	Yes (unlimited amount if in furtherance of tax-exempt purposes)
Must apply with the IRS.	Yes	No

Source: Draft Advocacy Guide Sheet and Internal Revenue Manual.

---

[5] Political campaign intervention is the term used in Treasury Regulations §§ 1.501(c)(3)-1, 1.501(c)(4)-1, 1.501(c)(5)-1, and 1.501(c)(6)-1.

[6] I.R.C. § 501(c)(5) (2012).

[7] I.R.C. § 501(c)(6) (2012).

[8] An organization engages in lobbying, or legislative activities, when it attempts to influence specific legislation by directly contacting members of a legislative body (Federal, State, or local) or encouraging the public to contact those members regarding that legislation. An organization also engages in lobbying when it encourages the public to take a position on a referendum. Lobbying is distinguished from political campaign intervention because lobbying does not involve attempts to influence the election of candidates for public office.

[9] An organization engages in general advocacy when it attempts to 1) influence public opinion on issues germane to the organization's tax-exempt purposes, 2) influence nonlegislative governing bodies (*e.g.*, the executive branch or regulatory agencies), or 3) encourage voter participation through "get out the vote" drives, voter guides, and candidate debates in a nonpartisan, neutral manner. General advocacy basically includes all types of advocacy other than political campaign intervention and lobbying.

During the 2012 election cycle, the activities of tax-exempt organizations received media coverage concerning the amount of money spent on influencing elections. According to the Center for Responsive Politics, tax-exempt groups, such as I.R.C. § 501(c)(4), I.R.C. § 501(c)(5), and I.R.C. § 501(c)(6) organizations, spent $133 million in Calendar Year 2010 on Federal candidate-oriented expenditures. In Calendar Year 2012, this figure increased to $315 million.[10] In addition, as shown in Figure 2, the number of applications for tax-exempt status has increased over the past four fiscal years.[11]

Figure 2: Number of Applications for I.R.C. §§ 501(c)(3)–(6) Tax-Exempt Status Received by the IRS

Fiscal Year	I.R.C. Subsection			
	501(c)(3)	501(c)(4)	501(c)(5)	501(c)(6)
2009	65,179	1,751	543	1,828
2010	59,486	1,735	290	1,637
2011	58,712	2,265	409	1,836
2012	66,543	3,357	1,081	2,338

Source: These data were provided by the EO function as background and were not validated for accuracy or reliability.

During the 2012 election cycle, some members of Congress raised concerns to the IRS about selective enforcement and the duty to treat similarly situated organizations consistently. In addition, several organizations applying for I.R.C. § 501(c)(4) tax-exempt status made allegations that the IRS 1) targeted specific groups applying for tax-exempt status, 2) delayed the processing of targeted groups' applications for tax-exempt status, and 3) requested unnecessary information from targeted organizations. Lastly, several members of Congress requested that the IRS investigate whether existing social welfare organizations are improperly engaged in a substantial, or even predominant, amount of campaign activity.

> *This audit focused on allegations that the IRS targeted specific groups applying for tax-exempt status, delayed the processing of targeted groups' applications, and requested unnecessary information from targeted organizations.*

We initiated this audit based on concerns expressed by Congress and reported in the media regarding the IRS's treatment of organizations applying for tax-exempt status. We focused our

---

[10] The Center for Responsive Politics obtained its information from the Federal Election Commission. We only included expenditures reported to the Federal Election Commission specifically for advocating the election or defeat of clearly identified Federal candidates.

[11] Some of this increase may be due to the reapplication of those organizations whose tax-exempt status was revoked as a result of not filing information returns for three consecutive years.

efforts on reviewing the processing of applications for tax-exempt status and determining whether allegations made against the IRS were founded.[12] Tax-exempt application case files were selected for review in June 2012 and were reviewed as provided by the EO function between July and November 2012. We did not review whether specific applications for tax-exempt status should be approved or denied.

This review was performed at the EO function Headquarters office in Washington, D.C., and the Determinations Unit in Cincinnati, Ohio, during the period June 2012 through February 2013. We conducted this performance audit in accordance with generally accepted government auditing standards. Those standards require that we plan and perform the audit to obtain sufficient, appropriate evidence to provide a reasonable basis for our findings and conclusions based on our audit objective. We believe that the evidence obtained provides a reasonable basis for our findings and conclusions based on our audit objective. Detailed information on our audit objective, scope, and methodology is presented in Appendix I. Major contributors to the report are listed in Appendix II.

---

[12] A future audit is being considered to assess how the EO function monitors I.R.C. §§ 501(c)(4)–(6) organizations to ensure that political campaign intervention does not constitute their primary activity.

Results of Review

The Determinations Unit Used Inappropriate Criteria to Identify Potential Political Cases

The Determinations Unit developed and used inappropriate criteria to identify applications from organizations with the words Tea Party in their names. These applications (hereafter referred to as potential political cases)[13] were forwarded to a team of specialists[14] for review. Subsequently, the Determinations Unit expanded the criteria to inappropriately include organizations with other specific names (Patriots and 9/12) or policy positions. While the criteria used by the Determinations Unit specified particular organization names, the team of specialists was also processing applications from groups with names other than those identified in the criteria. The inappropriate and changing criteria may have led to inconsistent treatment of organizations applying for tax-exempt status. For example, we identified some organizations' applications with evidence of significant political campaign intervention that were not forwarded to the team of specialists for processing but should have been. We also identified applications that were forwarded to the team of specialists but did not have indications of significant political campaign intervention. All applications that were forwarded to the team of specialists experienced substantial delays in processing. Although the IRS has taken some action, it will need to do more so that the public has reasonable assurance that applications are processed without unreasonable delay in a fair and impartial manner in the future.

Criteria for selecting applications inappropriately identified organizations based on their names and policy positions

The Determinations Unit developed and began using criteria to identify potential political cases for review that inappropriately identified specific groups applying for tax-exempt status based on their names or policy positions instead of developing criteria based on tax-exempt laws and Treasury Regulations.

***************************************1***
***************************************1***
*1***. According to media reports, some organizations were classified as I.R.C. § 501(c)(4) social welfare organizations but operated like political organizations. ********1**********

---

[13] Until July 2011, the Rulings and Agreements office referred to these cases as Tea Party cases. Afterwards, the EO function referred to these cases as advocacy cases.

[14] Initially, the team consisted of one specialist, but it was expanded to several specialists in December 2011. The EO function referred to this team as the advocacy team.

1. Soon thereafter, according to the IRS, a Determinations Unit specialist was asked to search for applications with Tea Party, Patriots, or 9/12 in the organization's name as well as other "political-sounding" names. EO function officials stated that, in May 2010, the Determinations Unit began developing a spreadsheet that would become known as the "Be On the Look Out" listing (hereafter referred to as the BOLO listing),[15] which included the emerging issue of Tea Party applications. In June 2010, the Determinations Unit began training its specialists on issues to be aware of, including Tea Party cases. By July 2010, Determinations Unit management stated that it had requested its specialists to be on the lookout for Tea Party applications.

In August 2010, the Determinations Unit distributed the first formal BOLO listing. The criteria in the BOLO listing were Tea Party organizations applying for I.R.C. § 501(c)(3) or I.R.C. § 501(c)(4) status. Based on our review of other BOLO listing criteria, the use of organization names on the BOLO listing is not unique to potential political cases.[16] EO function officials stated that Determinations Unit specialists interpreted the general criteria in the BOLO listing and developed expanded criteria for identifying potential political cases.[17] Figure 3 shows that, by June 2011, the expanded criteria included additional names (Patriots and 9/12 Project) as well as policy positions espoused by organizations in their applications.

Figure 3: Criteria for Potential Political Cases (June 2011)

"Tea Party," "Patriots" or "9/12 Project" is referenced in the case file
Issues include government spending, government debt or taxes
Education of the public by advocacy/lobbying to "make America a better place to live"
Statement in the case file criticize how the country is being run

Source: EO function briefing dated June 2011.

The mission of the IRS is to provide America's taxpayers top quality service by helping them understand and meet their tax responsibilities and by applying the tax law with integrity and fairness to all. According to IRS Policy Statement 1-1, IRS employees accomplish this mission by being impartial and handling tax matters in a manner that will promote public confidence. However, the criteria developed by the Determinations Unit gives the appearance that the IRS is not impartial in conducting its mission. The criteria focused narrowly on the names and policy

---

[15] The BOLO listing includes a consolidated list of emerging issues the EO function identifies for dissemination to Determinations Unit specialists.

[16] We did not review the use of other named organizations on the BOLO listing to determine if their use was appropriate.

[17] During interviews with Determinations Unit specialists and managers, we could not specifically determine who had been involved in creating the criteria. EO function officials later clarified that the expanded criteria were a compilation of various Determinations Unit specialists' responses on how they were identifying Tea Party cases.

positions of organizations instead of tax-exempt laws and Treasury Regulations. Criteria for selecting applications for the team of specialists should focus on the activities of the organizations and whether they fulfill the requirements of the law. Using the names or policy positions of organizations is not an appropriate basis for identifying applications for review by the team of specialists.

We asked the Acting Commissioner, Tax Exempt and Government Entities Division; the Director, EO; and Determinations Unit personnel if the criteria were influenced by any individual or organization outside the IRS. All of these officials stated that the criteria were not influenced by any individual or organization outside the IRS. Instead, the Determinations Unit developed and implemented inappropriate criteria in part due to insufficient oversight provided by management. Specifically, only first-line management approved references to the Tea Party in the BOLO listing criteria before it was implemented. As a result, inappropriate criteria remained in place for more than 18 months. Determinations Unit employees also did not consider the public perception of using politically sensitive criteria when identifying these cases. Lastly, the criteria developed showed a lack of knowledge in the Determinations Unit of what activities are allowed by I.R.C. § 501(c)(3) and I.R.C. § 501(c)(4) organizations.

Determinations Unit employees stated that they considered the Tea Party criterion as a shorthand term for all potential political cases. Whether the inappropriate criterion was shorthand for all potential political cases or not, developing and using criteria that focuses on organization names and policy positions instead of the activities permitted under the Treasury Regulations does not promote public confidence that tax-exempt laws are being adhered to impartially. In addition, the applications for those organizations that were identified for processing by the team of specialists experienced significant delays and requests for unnecessary information that is detailed later in this report.

After being briefed on the expanded criteria in June 2011, the Director, EO, immediately directed that the criteria be changed. In July 2011, the criteria were changed to focus on the potential "political, lobbying, or [general] advocacy" activities of the organization. These criteria were an improvement over using organization names and policy positions. However, the team of specialists subsequently changed the criteria in January 2012 without executive approval because they believed the July 2011 criteria were too broad. The January 2012 criteria again focused on the policy positions of organizations instead of tax-exempt laws and Treasury Regulations. After three months, the Director, Rulings and Agreements, learned the criteria had been changed by the team of specialists and subsequently revised the criteria again in May 2012. (See Appendix VI for a complete timeline of criteria used to identify potential political cases). The May 2012 criteria more clearly focus on activities permitted under the Treasury Regulations. As a result of changes made to the criteria without management knowledge, the Director, Rulings and Agreements, issued a memorandum requiring all original entries and changes to criteria included on the BOLO listing be approved at the executive level prior to implementation.

The team of specialists processed applications by organizations with names other than Tea Party, Patriots, and 9/12

To determine if organizations other than those specifically identified in the inappropriate criteria were processed by the team of specialists, we reviewed the names on all applications identified as potential political cases.[18] Figure 4 shows that approximately one-third of the applications identified for processing by the team of specialists included Tea Party, Patriots, or 9/12 in their names, while the remainder did not. According to the Director, Rulings and Agreements, the fact that the team of specialists worked applications that did not involve the Tea Party, Patriots, or 9/12 groups demonstrated that the IRS was not politically biased in its identification of applications for processing by the team of specialists.

Figure 4: Breakdown of Potential Political Cases by Organization Name

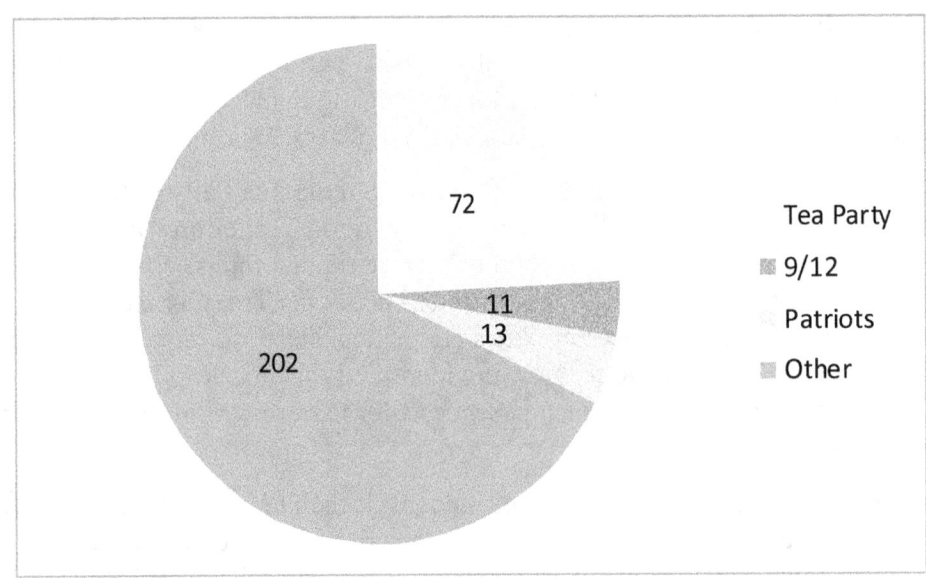

Source: EO function Potential Political Case Tracking Sheet as of May 31, 2012.

While the team of specialists reviewed applications from a variety of organizations, we determined during our reviews of statistical samples of I.R.C. § 501(c)(4) tax-exempt applications that all cases with Tea Party, Patriots, or 9/12 in their names were forwarded to the team of specialists.[19]

---

[18] We could not determine which potential political cases may have been identified based on an organization's policy positions.

[19] We determined this through two statistical samples of 338 (7.5 percent) from a universe of 4,510 I.R.C. § 501(c)(4) tax-exempt applications filed during May 2010 through May 2012 that were not forwarded to the team of specialists. See Appendix I for details on our sampling methodology.

Some applications with indications of significant political campaign intervention were not identified for review by the team of specialists

In May 2012, the Director, Rulings and Agreements, approved the current criteria for identifying potential political cases. The criteria are "501(c)(3), 501(c)(4), 501(c)(5), and 501(c)(6) organizations with indicators of significant amounts of political campaign intervention...." To determine if all cases with indications of significant political campaign intervention were sent to the team of specialists, we reviewed two statistical samples of I.R.C. § 501(c)(4) applications.

- **Applications That the IRS Determined Required Minimal or No Additional Information for Processing** – We reviewed a statistical sample of 94 I.R.C. § 501(c)(4) cases closed from May 2010[20] through May 2012 from a universe of 2,051 applications that the IRS determined required minimal or no additional information from the organizations (also referred to by the EO function as merit closures). We determined that two (2 percent) of 94 approved applications had indications of significant political campaign intervention and should have been forwarded to the team of specialists.[21] Based on our statistical sample, we project an estimated 44 merit closure applications were not appropriately identified as potential political cases during this time period.[22]

- **Applications Identified by the IRS That Required Additional Information for Processing** – We reviewed a statistical sample of 244 I.R.C. § 501(c)(4) cases closed from May 2010 through May 2012 or open as of May 31, 2012, from a universe of 2,459 applications that the IRS determined required additional information from the organizations applying for tax-exempt status (also referred to by the EO function as full development applications) but were not forwarded to the team of specialists. For the applications that were available for our review, we found that 14 (6 percent)[23] of 237 applications[24] included indications of significant political campaign intervention and should have been processed by the team of specialists.[25] We project an estimated 141 full development applications were not appropriately identified as potential political cases during this time period.[26]

---

[20] May 2010 was chosen because it is the first date that we were informed that the Determinations Unit was using criteria which identified specific organizations by name.

[21] Neither of the two cases involved a Tea Party, Patriots, or 9/12 organization.

[22] See Appendix IV.

[23] None of the 14 cases involved a Tea Party, Patriots, or 9/12 organization.

[24] We could not analyze seven sampled application case files because of incomplete documentation in the case files (six applications) or the case file could not be located (one application). See Appendix IV.

[25] We determined that eight applications were appropriately forwarded to the team of specialists. Five of the eight application case files involved Tea Party, Patriots, or 9/12 organizations.

[26] See Appendix IV.

To determine if cases without indications of significant political campaign intervention were sent to the team of specialists, we reviewed all of the applications identified as potential political cases as of May 31, 2012.

- **Applications That the IRS Determined Should Be Processed by the Team of Specialists** – We reviewed all 298 applications that had been identified as potential political cases as of May 31, 2012. In the majority of cases, we agreed that the applications submitted included indications of significant political campaign intervention. However, we did not identify any indications of significant political campaign intervention for 91 (31 percent) of the 296 applications[27] that had complete documentation.[28]

We discussed our results with EO function officials, who disagreed with our findings. Although EO function officials provided explanations about why the applications should have been identified as potential political cases, the case files did not include the specific reason(s) the applications were selected. EO function officials also stated that applications may not literally include statements indicating significant political campaign intervention.[29] According to EO function officials, organizations may not understand what constitutes political campaign intervention or may provide vague descriptions of certain activities that the EO function knows from past experience potentially involve political campaign intervention. In these cases, the EO function believes it is important to review the applications to ensure that political campaign intervention is not the organizations' primary activity. To provide further assurance that Determinations Unit employees are handling tax matters in an impartial manner, it would be helpful to document specifically why applications are chosen for further review.

Recommendations

The Director, EO, should:

Recommendation 1: Ensure that the memorandum requiring the Director, Rulings and Agreements, to approve all original entries and changes to criteria included on the BOLO listing prior to implementation be formalized in the appropriate Internal Revenue Manual.

> **Management's Response:** The IRS agreed with this recommendation and will ensure that the procedures set forth in the memorandum requiring the Director,

---

[27] We could not complete our review of two cases due to inadequate documentation in the case files. See Appendix IV.

[28] Seventeen (19 percent) of the 91 applications involved Tea Party, Patriots, or 9/12 organizations.

[29] It should also be noted that, in some cases, specialists obtained additional information after the application was received that indicated the organizations were involved in political campaign intervention which was not available in the initial application documentation we reviewed.

Rulings and Agreements, to approve in advance all original entries and changes to the BOLO listing are made part of the Internal Revenue Manual.

Recommendation 2: Develop procedures to better document the reason(s) applications are chosen for review by the team of specialists (*e.g.*, evidence of specific political campaign intervention in the application file or specific reasons the EO function may have for choosing to review the application further based on past experience).

> **Management's Response:** The IRS proposed an alternative corrective action to our recommendation. The IRS stated it will review its screening procedures to determine whether, and to what extent, additional documentation can be implemented without having an adverse impact on the timeliness of case processing.

> **Office of Audit Comment:** We do not believe this alternative corrective action fully addresses the recommendation. Developing procedures to better document the reasons applications are chosen for further review would help ensure that applications are being handled in an impartial manner. In addition, as detailed in the next section of this report, the average time these applications have been open is 574 days as of December 17, 2012. We do not believe documenting a brief explanation about why applications are chosen for review would have an adverse impact on the timeliness of case processing.

Recommendation 3: Develop training or workshops to be held before each election cycle including, but not limited to, the proper ways to identify applications that require review of political campaign intervention activities.

> **Management's Response:** The IRS agreed with this recommendation and will develop training on the topics described in Recommendations 3, 5, 6, and 9. Because election cycles are continuous, the IRS will develop a schedule which ensures that staff have the training as needed to handle potential political intervention matters.

Potential Political Cases Experienced Significant Processing Delays

Organizations that applied for tax-exempt status and had their applications forwarded to the team of specialists experienced substantial delays. As of December 17, 2012, many organizations had not received an approval or denial letter for more than two years after they submitted their applications. Some cases have been open during two election cycles (2010 and 2012). The *IRS Strategic Plan 2009–2013* has several goals and objectives that involve timely interacting with taxpayers, including enforcement of the tax law in a timely manner while minimizing taxpayer burden. The EO function does not have specific timeliness goals for processing applications, such as potential political cases, that require significant follow-up with the organizations.[30] The time it takes to process an application depends upon the facts and circumstances of the case.

Potential political cases took significantly longer than average to process due to ineffective management oversight. Once cases were initially identified for processing by the team of specialists, the Determinations Unit Program Manager requested assistance via e-mail from the Technical Unit to ensure consistency in processing the cases. However, EO function management did not ensure that there was a formal process in place for initiating, tracking, or monitoring requests for assistance. In addition, there were several changes in Rulings and Agreements management responsible for overseeing the fulfillment of requests for assistance from the Determinations Unit during this time period. This contributed to the lengthy delays in processing potential political cases. As a result, the Determinations Unit waited more than 20 months (February 2010 to November 2011) to receive draft written guidance from the Technical Unit for processing potential political cases.

As a result, the IRS delayed the issuance of letters to organizations approving their tax-exempt status. For I.R.C. § 501(c)(3) organizations, this means that potential donors and grantors could be reluctant to provide donations or grants.[31] In addition, some organizations withdrew their applications and others may not have begun conducting planned charitable or social welfare work. The delays may have also prevented some organizations from receiving certain benefits of the tax-exempt status. For example, if organizations are approved for tax-exempt status, they may receive exemption from certain State taxes and reduced postal rates. For organizations that may eventually be denied tax-exempt status but have been operating while their applications are pending, the organizations will be required to retroactively file income tax returns and may be liable to pay income taxes for, in some cases, more than two years.

To analyze the delays, we: 1) reviewed the events that led to delays in processing potential political cases, 2) compared the amount of time cases assigned to the team of specialists were open to applications that were not assigned to the team of specialists, and 3) determined if organizations were eligible to sue the IRS due to delays in processing certain applications.

Potential political cases experienced long processing delays

The team of specialists stopped working on potential political cases from October 2010 through November 2011, resulting in a 13-month delay, while they waited for assistance from the Technical Unit. Figure 5 illustrates significant events and delays concerning potential political cases. For a comprehensive timeline of events related to potential political cases, see Appendix VII.

---

[30] The EO function, however, had an overall goal to process merit and full development tax-exempt applications in 121 days for Fiscal Year 2012.
[31] Of 298 cases reviewed, 89 were I.R.C. § 501(c)(3) organizations.

Figure 5: Timeline of Events and Delays Involving the Processing of Potential Political Cases (***1******* Through May 2012)**

Date	Events and Delays
******1******	*******************************1********************************* *******************1*********.
April 2010	The team of specialists is formed with one specialist who is assigned potential political cases and begins working on them with the assistance of a Technical Unit employee.
October 2010	The team of specialists stops processing potential political cases while waiting for assistance from the Technical Unit.
July 2011	The EO function decides to develop written guidance for the Determinations Unit to process the potential political cases.
November 2011	Draft written guidance is provided to the Determinations Unit.
December 2011	Additional specialists are added to the team of specialists.
January 2012	Specialists begin issuing additional information request letters to organizations applying for tax-exempt status, requesting that the information be provided in two to three weeks. These time periods are standard response times given for any information request and are included in the Internal Revenue Manual.
February 2012	Concerns are raised in the media regarding requests for significant amounts of information from organizations applying for tax-exempt status. The Director, EO, stops specialists from issuing any more letters requesting information. Instead, letters allowing extensions of 60 days to respond to previous additional information letters were developed and issued in March and April 2012. These letters also noted that applicants should contact the IRS if they needed longer than 60 days to respond.
May 2012	A workshop is given to Determinations Unit specialists assigned to potential political cases. Afterwards, a review of all the open cases is completed to recommend whether additional processing is necessary or whether the cases can be closed (as of December 17, 2012, 160 applications were still being processed).

Source: *Interviews of EO function employees and our review of EO function e-mails.*

Ineffective oversight by management led to significant delays in processing potential political cases. **1***************************** ***********1*******************************. In April 2010, the Determinations Unit Program Manager requested via e-mail a contact in the Technical Unit to provide assistance with processing the applications. A Technical Unit specialist was assigned this task and began working with the team of specialists. The team of specialists stopped processing cases in October 2010 without closing any of the 40 cases that were begun. However, the Determinations Unit Program Manager thought the cases were being processed. Later, we were informed by the Director, Rulings and Agreements, that there was a miscommunication about processing the cases. The Determinations Unit waited for assistance from the Technical Unit instead of continuing to process the cases. The Determinations Unit Program Manager requested status updates on the request for assistance several times via e-mail. Draft written guidance was not received from the Technical Unit until November 2011, 13 months after the Determinations Unit stopped processing the cases. As of the end of our audit work in February 2013, the guidance had not been finalized because the EO function decided to provide training instead.[32]

Many organizations waited much longer than 13 months for a decision, while others have yet to receive a decision from the IRS. For example, as of December 17, 2012, the IRS had been processing several potential political cases for more than 1,000 calendar days. Some of these organizations received requests for additional information in Calendar Year 2010 and then did not hear from the IRS again for more than a year while the Determinations Unit waited for assistance from the Technical Unit. For the 296 potential political cases we reviewed,[33] as of December 17, 2012, 108 applications had been approved, 28 were withdrawn by the applicant, none had been denied, and 160 cases were open from 206 to 1,138 calendar days (some crossing two election cycles).

In March 2012, the Deputy Commissioner, Services and Enforcement, asked the Senior Technical Advisor to the Acting Commissioner, Tax Exempt and Government Entities Division, to look into concerns raised by the media about delays in processing applications for tax-exempt status from Tea Party groups and the nature of the questions being asked related to the applications. In April 2012, the Senior Technical Advisor to the Acting Commissioner, Tax Exempt and Government Entities Division, along with a team of EO function Headquarters office employees, reviewed many of the potential political cases and determined that there appeared to be some confusion by Determinations Unit specialists and applicants on what activities are allowed by I.R.C. § 501(c)(4) organizations. We believe this could be due to the lack of specific guidance on how to determine the "primary activity" of an I.R.C. § 501(c)(4) organization. Treasury Regulations state that I.R.C. § 501(c)(4) organizations should have social welfare as their "primary activity"; however, the regulations do not define how to measure whether social welfare is an organization's "primary activity."

As a result of this confusion, the EO function Headquarters employees provided a two-day workshop to the team of specialists in May 2012 to train them on what activities are allowable by I.R.C. § 501(c)(4) organizations, including lobbying and political campaign intervention. After this workshop, potential political cases were independently reviewed by two people to determine what, if any, additional work needed to be completed prior to making a decision to approve or deny the applications for tax-exempt status. This review continued on any newly identified potential political cases. Prior to the hands-on training and independent reviews, the team of specialists had only approved six (2 percent) of 298 applications. After the hands-on training

---

[32] In response to the National Taxpayer Advocate's *2007 Annual Report to Congress*, the IRS commented that putting guide sheets for processing applications for tax-exempt status on its Internet site would result in fewer delays.

[33] ***|**.

and independent reviews began, the Determinations Unit approved an additional 102 applications by December 2012.[34] In addition, it was decided that applications could be approved, but a referral for follow-up could be sent to another unit,[35] which could review the activities of an organization at a later date to determine if they were consistent with the organization's tax-exempt status.

Potential political cases were open much longer than similar cases that were not identified for processing by the team of specialists

For Fiscal Year 2012, the average time it took the Determinations Unit to complete processing applications requiring additional information from organizations applying for tax-exempt status (also referred to by the EO function as full development cases) was 238 calendar days according to IRS data. In comparison, the average time a potential political case was open as of December 17, 2012, was 574 calendar days (with 158 potential political cases being open longer than the average calendar days it took to close other full development cases).[36] Figure 6 shows that more than 80 percent of the potential political cases have been open more than one year.

Figure 6: Number of Calendar Days Potential Political Cases Were Open (as of December 17, 2012)

	Number and Percentage[37] of Potential Political Cases Open by Calendar Day Range				
Total Cases	0–120 Calendar Days	121–180 Calendar Days	181–270 Calendar Days	271–365 Calendar Days	More Than 365 Calendar Days
160	0 (0%)	0 (0%)	3 (2%)	28 (18%)	129 (81%)

Source: Our analysis of EO function documentation.

---

[34] Of the 102 applications, 29 (28 percent) involved Tea Party, Patriots, or 9/12 organizations.

[35] The Review of Operations Unit completes compliance reviews on tax-exempt organizations to determine whether they are operating in accordance with their tax-exempt purposes and are current with their filing requirements. Unit personnel review information available on IRS systems, filed returns, applications for tax exemption, and the Internet to assess the organizations' operations and make recommendations for further actions.

[36] See Appendix IV.

[37] Percentages may not equal 100 percent due to rounding.

Some charitable organizations were eligible to sue the IRS for declaratory judgment due to the delays in processing applications

The Determinations Unit did not always timely approve or deny the applications for I.R.C. § 501(c)(3) tax-exempt status for potential political cases. However, the tax law provides organizations with the ability to sue the IRS to force a decision on their applications if the IRS does not approve or deny their applications within 270 calendar days.[38]

As of May 31, 2012,[39] 32 (36 percent) of 89 I.R.C. § 501(c)(3) potential political cases were open more than 270 calendar days, and the organizations had responded timely to all requests for additional information, as required. As of the end of our fieldwork, none of these organizations had sued the IRS, even though they had the legal right. In another 38 open cases, organizations were timely in their responses to additional information requests, but the 270-calendar-day threshold had not been reached as of May 31, 2012. These 38 organizations may have the right to sue the IRS in the future if determinations are not made within the 270-calendar-day period.

Recommendations

The Director, EO, should:

Recommendation 4: Develop a process for the Determinations Unit to formally request assistance from the Technical Unit and the Guidance Unit.[40] The process should include actions to initiate, track, and monitor requests for assistance to ensure that requests are responded to timely.

> **Management's Response:** The IRS agreed with this recommendation and will develop a formal process for the Determination Unit to request assistance and to monitor such requests.

Recommendation 5: Develop guidance for specialists on how to process requests for tax-exempt status involving potentially significant political campaign intervention. This guidance should also be posted to the Internet to provide transparency to organizations on the application process.

> **Management's Response:** The IRS proposed alternative corrective action to our recommendation. The IRS will develop training on the topics described in Recommendations 3, 5, 6, and 9. Because election cycles are continuous, the IRS

---

[38] Revenue Procedure 2012-09 provides further guidance on the implementation of this right.

[39] Tax-exempt application case files were selected for review in June 2012 based on a May 31, 2012, listing of applications being processed by the team of specialists.

[40] The Guidance Unit provides formal and informal guidance that explains how certain laws, such as regulations, revenue rulings, revenue procedures, notices, and announcements, may apply to exempt organizations.

noted that it will develop a schedule which ensures that staff have the training as needed to handle potential political intervention matters.

> ***Office of Audit Comment:*** We do not believe that this alternative corrective action fully addresses our recommendation. We believe that specific guidance should be developed and made available to specialists processing potential political cases. Making this guidance available on the Internet for organizations could also address a concern raised in the IRS's response that many applications appear to contain incomplete and inconsistent information.

Recommendation 6: Develop training or workshops to be held before each election cycle including, but not limited to: a) what constitutes political campaign intervention versus general advocacy (including case examples) and b) the ability to refer for follow-up those organizations that may conduct activities in a future year which may cause them to lose their tax-exempt status.

> ***Management's Response:*** The IRS agreed with this recommendation and will develop training on the topics described in Recommendations 3, 5, 6, and 9. Because election cycles are continuous, the IRS reported that it will develop a schedule which ensures that staff have the training as needed to handle potential political intervention matters.

Recommendation 7: Provide oversight to ensure that potential political cases, some of which have been in process for three years, are approved or denied expeditiously.

> ***Management's Response:*** The IRS agreed with this recommendation and stated that, while this is an ongoing project, it is closely overseeing the remaining open cases to ensure that it reaches determinations as expeditiously as possible.

The Acting Commissioner, Tax Exempt and Government Entities Division, should:

Recommendation 8: Recommend to IRS Chief Counsel and the Department of the Treasury that guidance on how to measure the "primary activity" of I.R.C. § 501(c)(4) social welfare organizations be included for consideration in the Department of the Treasury Priority Guidance Plan.[41]

> ***Management's Response:*** The IRS agreed with this recommendation and will share this recommendation with the IRS Chief Counsel and the Department of Treasury's Office of Tax Policy.

---

[41] The Department of the Treasury issues a Priority Guidance Plan each year to identify and prioritize the tax issues that should be addressed through regulations, revenue rulings, revenue procedures, notices, and other published administrative guidance.

The Determinations Unit Requested Unnecessary Information for Many Potential Political Cases

The Determinations Unit sent requests for information that we later (in whole or in part) determined to be unnecessary for 98 (58 percent) of 170 organizations that received additional information request letters.[42] According to the Internal Revenue Manual, these requests should be thorough, complete, and relevant. However, the Determinations Unit requested irrelevant (unnecessary) information because of a lack of managerial review, at all levels, of questions before they were sent to organizations seeking tax-exempt status. We also believe that Determinations Unit specialists lacked knowledge of what activities are allowed by I.R.C. § 501(c)(3) and I.R.C. § 501(c)(4) tax-exempt organizations. This created burden on the organizations that were required to gather and forward information that was not needed by the Determinations Unit and led to delays in processing the applications. These delays could result in potential donors and grantors being reluctant to provide donations or grants to organizations applying for I.R.C. § 501(c)(3) tax-exempt status. In addition, some organizations may not have begun conducting planned charitable or social welfare work.

After receiving draft guidance in November 2011, the team of specialists began sending requests for additional information in January 2012 to organizations that were applying for tax-exempt status. For some organizations, this was the second letter received from the IRS requesting additional information, the first of which had been received more than a year before this date. These letters requested that the information be provided in two or three weeks (as is customary in these letters) despite the fact that the IRS had done nothing with some of the applications for more than one year. After the letters were received, organizations seeking tax-exempt status, as well as members of Congress, expressed concerns about the type and extent of questions being asked. For example, the Determinations Unit requested donor information from 27 organizations[43] that it would be required to make public if the application was approved, even though this information could not be disclosed by the IRS when provided by organizations whose tax-exempt status had been approved. Figure 7 shows an example of requests sent to organizations applying for tax-exempt status regarding donors.

---

[42] See Appendix IV.
[43] Of the 27 organizations, 13 had Tea Party, Patriots, or 9/12 in their names.

**Figure 7: Example of Requests for Information Regarding
Past and Future Donors in Letters Sent in January/February 2012**

Provide the following information for the income you received and raised for the years from inception to the present. Also, provide the same information for the income you expect to receive and raise for 2012, 2013, and 2014.

 a. Donations, contributions, and grant income for each year, which includes the following information:

   1. The names of the donors, contributors, and grantors. If the donor, contributor, or grantor has run or will run for a public office, identify the office. If not, please confirm by answering this question "No."

   2. The amounts of each of the donations, contributions, and grants and the dates you received them.

   3. How did you use these donations, contributions, and grants? Provide the details.

If you did not receive or do not expect to receive any donation, contribution, and grant income, please confirm by answering "None received" and/or "None expected."

Source: Application case files.

After media attention, the Director, EO, stopped issuance of additional information request letters and provided an extension of time to respond to previously issued letters. The Deputy Commissioner for Services and Enforcement then asked the Senior Technical Advisor to the Acting Commissioner, Tax Exempt and Government Entities Division, to find out how applications were being processed and make recommendations. The Senior Technical Advisor and a team of specialists visited the Determinations Unit in Cincinnati, Ohio, and began reviewing cases. As part of this effort, EO function Headquarters office employees reviewed the additional information request letters prepared by the team of specialists and identified seven questions that they deemed unnecessary. Subsequently, the EO function instituted the practice that all additional information request letters for potential political cases be reviewed by the EO function Headquarters office before they are sent to organizations seeking tax-exempt status. In addition, EO function officials informed us that they decided to destroy all donor lists that were sent in for potential political cases that the IRS determined it should not have requested. Figure 8 lists the seven questions identified as being unnecessary.

Figure 8: Seven Questions Identified As Unnecessary by the EO Function

Number	Question
1	Requests the names of donors.
2	Requests a list of all issues that are important to the organization and asks that the organization indicate its position regarding such issues.
3	Requests 1) the roles and activities of the audience and participants other than members in the activity and 2) the type of conversations and discussions members and participants had during the activity.
4	Asks whether the officer, director, *etc.*, has run or will run for public office.
5	Requests the political affiliation of the officer, director, speakers, candidates supported, *etc.*, or otherwise refers to the relationship with identified political party–related organizations.
6	Requests information regarding employment, other than for the organization, including hours worked.
7	Requests information regarding activities of another organization – not just the relationship of the other organization to the applicant.

Source: EO function review of additional information request letters.

We reviewed case file information for all 170 organizations that received additional information request letters and determined that 98 (58 percent) had received requests for information that was later deemed unnecessary by the EO function. Of the 98 organizations:

- 15 were informed that they did not need to respond to previous requests for information and, instead, received a revised request for information.

- 12 either received a letter or a telephone call stating that their application was approved and they no longer needed to respond to information requests they had received from the IRS.

Figure 9 shows excerpts from the approval letter developed for organizations that did not need to respond to a previous additional information request letter.

Figure 9: Excerpts From a Template Approval Letter, Which Includes a Statement That Previously Requested Information Is No Longer Needed

> **Dear Applicant:**
>
> **We are pleased to inform you that upon review of your application for tax-exempt status we have determined that you are exempt from Federal income tax under section 501 (c) (4) of the Internal Revenue Code. Because this letter could help resolve any questions regarding your exempt status, you should keep it in your permanent records.**

> **Please not that we have just completed another review of your request to be recognized as tax-exempt under section 501 (c) (4) of the Internal Revenue Codes. Based on that review, we concluded that we do not need the additional materials previously requested because your application and materials provide sufficient information.**

Source: IRS template approval letter.

Recommendation

Recommendation 9: The Director, EO, should develop training or workshops to be held before each election cycle including, but not limited to, how to word questions in additional information request letters and what additional information should be requested.

> **Management's Response:** The IRS agreed with this recommendation and will develop training on the topics described in Recommendations 3, 5, 6, and 9. Because election cycles are continuous, the IRS reported that it will develop a schedule which ensures that staff have the training as needed to handle potential political intervention matters.

Appendix I

Detailed Objective, Scope, and Methodology

The overall objective was to determine whether allegations were founded that the IRS:
1) targeted specific groups applying for tax-exempt status, 2) delayed processing targeted
groups' applications for tax-exempt status, and 3) requested unnecessary information from
targeted groups. To accomplish our objective, we:

I. Assessed the actions taken by the EO function in response to the increase in applications
for tax-exempt status from organizations potentially involved in political campaign
intervention.

    A. Interviewed EO function management to identify steps taken and who authorized
them. We also developed a timeline of events.

    B. Obtained a list of applications that were identified for processing by the team of
specialists and determined the status of the identified cases (open, approved, denied,
etc.) through May 31, 2012. We also received an updated list of identified cases
through December 17, 2012, to determine the status of each initial case as of this date.

    C. Determined whether procedures and controls in place since May 2010 resulted in
inconsistent treatment of applications potentially involving political campaign
intervention.

II. Determined whether changes to procedures and controls since May 2010 affected the
timeliness of reviewing applications potentially involving political campaign
intervention.

    A. Interviewed EO function personnel to determine whether there were any outside
influences that affected the timeliness of reviewing potential political cases.

    B. Reviewed all 89 I.R.C. § 501(c)(3) potential political cases to determine whether they
were processed within the 270-day standard required by law.

III. Determined whether the actions taken by the EO function to identify applications for
tax-exempt status of organizations potentially involved in political campaign intervention
were consistent.

    A. Selected a statistical sample of 244 open and closed I.R.C. § 501(c)(4) application
cases from a universe of 2,459 cases that the IRS determined needed significant
additional information (full development) on the Employee Plans/Exempt
Organizations Determination System from May 2010 through May 2012 to determine
whether they should have been identified for processing by the team of specialists.

We selected our statistical sample using the following criteria: 90 percent confidence level, 50 percent error rate,[1] and ± 5 percent precision rate. We used a random sample to ensure that each application case had an equal chance of being selected, which enabled us to obtain sufficient evidence to support our results. A contracted statistician reviewed our projections.

1. Obtained the universe of 2,459 cases from the Employee Plans/Exempt Organizations Determination System and performed validity checks to ensure that the data were accurate. We found the data could be relied on for this review.

2. Obtained a statistical sample of open and closed application cases.

3. Determined whether application cases with potential political campaign intervention issues were identified for processing by the team of specialists.

4. Interviewed EO function personnel to obtain their perspective on any application cases we identified that should have been identified for processing by the team of specialists but were not.

B. Selected a statistical sample of 94 closed I.R.C. § 501(c)(4) application cases from a universe of 2,051 cases that the IRS determined did not need significant additional information (merit cases) on the Employee Plans/Exempt Organizations Determination System from May 2010 through May 2012 to determine whether they should have been identified for processing by the team of specialists. We selected our statistical sample using the following criteria: 90 percent confidence level, 10 percent error rate,[2] and ± 5 percent precision rate. We used a random sample to ensure that each application case had an equal chance of being selected, which enabled us to obtain sufficient evidence to support our results. A contracted statistician reviewed our projections.

1. Obtained the universe of 2,051 cases from the Employee Plans/Exempt Organizations Determination System and performed validity checks to ensure that the data were accurate. We found the data could be relied on for this review.

2. Obtained a statistical sample of closed application cases.

3. Determined whether application cases with potential political campaign intervention issues were not identified for processing by the team of specialists.

---

[1] An expected error rate of 50 percent was chosen because we determined that cases needing significant additional information had criteria that included the names of specific groups.
[2] An expected error rate of 10 percent was chosen because procedures require that cases with political issues generally need significant additional information.

4. Interviewed EO function personnel to obtain their perspective on any applications we identified that should have been identified for processing by the team of specialists but were not.

C. Obtained and reviewed all 298 application cases identified for processing by the team of specialists as of May 31, 2012, to determine whether they were correctly identified.

1. Determined whether application cases were correctly identified for processing by the team of specialists.

2. Interviewed EO function personnel to obtain their perspective on any cases we identified that should not have been identified for processing by the team of specialists.

D. Computed the average cycle time of processing potential political cases and compared it to the average cycle time for processing similar cases that were not processed by the team of specialists.

E. Determined the number of organizations that may have been adversely affected by inconsistent treatment.

IV. Determined whether the EO function consistently had a reasonable basis for requesting information from organizations seeking tax-exempt status that were potentially involved in political campaign intervention.

A. Reviewed all 170 potential political cases that were issued additional information request letters to determine whether the letters included questions deemed unnecessary by the EO function.

B. Interviewed EO function personnel to obtain their perspective on additional information that was requested that may not have been necessary to help make a determination decision.

C. Determined the number of taxpayers that may have been adversely affected.

Internal controls methodology

Internal controls relate to management's plans, methods, and procedures used to meet their mission, goals, and objectives. Internal controls include the processes and procedures for planning, organizing, directing, and controlling program operations. They include the systems for measuring, reporting, and monitoring program performance. We determined the following internal controls were relevant to our audit objective: EO function policies, procedures, and practices for identifying and processing applications for tax-exempt status with indications of political campaign intervention. We evaluated these controls by interviewing personnel, reviewing documentation, reviewing statistical samples of applications for tax-exempt status, and reviewing applications identified as involving potential political campaign intervention.

Appendix II

Major Contributors to This Report

Gregory D. Kutz, Assistant Inspector General for Audit (Management Services and Exempt Organizations)
Russell P. Martin, Acting Assistant Inspector General for Audit (Management Services and Exempt Organizations)
Troy D. Paterson, Director
Thomas F. Seidell, Audit Manager
Cheryl J. Medina, Lead Auditor
Julia Moore, Senior Auditor
Michael A. McGovern, Auditor
Evan A. Close, Audit Evaluator

Appendix III

Report Distribution List

Acting Commissioner C
Office of the Commissioner – Attn: Chief of Staff C
Chief Counsel CC
Deputy Commissioner for Services and Enforcement SE
National Taxpayer Advocate TA
Acting Deputy Commissioner, Tax Exempt and Government Entities Division SE:T
Director, Exempt Organizations, Tax Exempt and Government Entities Division SE:T:EO
Director, Office of Legislative Affairs CL:LA
Director, Office of Program Evaluation and Risk Analysis RAS:O
Office of Internal Control OS:CFO:CPIC:IC
Audit Liaison: Director, Communications and Liaison, Tax Exempt and Government Entities
Division SE:T:CL

Appendix IV

Outcome Measures

This appendix presents detailed information on the measurable impact that our recommended corrective actions will have on tax administration. These benefits will be incorporated into our Semiannual Report to Congress.

Type and Value of Outcome Measure:

- Reliability of Information – Actual; nine application case files that were either incomplete or could not be located for us to review (see page 5).

Methodology Used to Measure the Reported Benefit:

During our review of applications for tax-exempt status that were not identified for the team of specialists, we were unable to review seven case files because the case file lacked complete documentation (six cases) or the case file could not be located (one case). In addition, during our review of all identified potential political cases through May 31, 2012, we were unable to analyze two case files because of incomplete documentation.

Type and Value of Outcome Measure:

- Reliability of Information – Potential; 44 organizations whose tax-exempt applications were not appropriately identified as having significant potential political campaign intervention (see page 5).

Methodology Used to Measure the Reported Benefit:

We selected a simple random sample of 94 I.R.C. § 501(c)(4) cases closed from May 2010 through May 2012 from a universe of 2,051 applications that the IRS determined required minimal or no additional information from organizations applying for tax-exempt status. During our case reviews, we determined that two cases were not appropriately identified as having significant potential political campaign intervention. We projected, with 90 percent confidence, an actual error rate of between 0.38 percent and 6.55 percent[1] and that between eight and 134 applications[2] were not properly identified for processing by the team of specialists.

---

[1] The point estimate error rate for the sample is 2.13 percent. The 90 percent confidence interval was calculated using the Exact Binomial Method.

[2] The point estimate number of error applications is 44. The 90 percent confidence interval was calculated using the Exact Binomial Method.

Type and Value of Outcome Measure:

- Reliability of Information – Potential; 141 organizations whose tax-exempt applications were not appropriately identified as having significant potential political campaign intervention (see page 5).

Methodology Used to Measure the Reported Benefit:

We selected a simple random sample of 244 I.R.C. § 501(c)(4) cases closed from May 2010 through May 2012 or open as of May 31, 2012, from a universe of 2,459 applications that the IRS determined required additional information from organizations applying for tax-exempt status.[3] During our case reviews, we determined that 14 cases were not appropriately identified as having significant potential political campaign intervention. We projected, with 90 percent confidence, an actual error rate of between 3.38 percent and 8.43 percent[4] and that between 84 and 198 applications[5] were not properly identified for processing by the team of specialists.

Type and Value of Outcome Measure:

- Taxpayer Burden – Potential; 158 organizations that waited longer than average for the IRS to make a decision regarding their tax-exempt status (see page 11).

Methodology Used to Measure the Reported Benefit:

We obtained data from the EO function on the average number of days it took to determine whether an application for tax-exempt status was approved or denied. In Fiscal Year 2012, it took on average 238 days to close a case that needed additional information from the organization prior to approving or denying the application. As of December 17, 2012, there were 158 potential political cases that were open more than 238 calendar days.

Type and Value of Outcome Measure:

- Taxpayer Burden – Potential; 98 organizations that received additional information request letters with questions that were later deemed unnecessary by the EO function (see page 18).

Methodology Used to Measure the Reported Benefit:

We reviewed 170 potential political cases that had received additional information request letters from the Determinations Unit. Using a list of seven questions/topics that the EO function categorized as unnecessary, we identified 98 potential political cases that included additional information request letters asking questions deemed unnecessary by the EO function.

---

[3] We found that seven cases from the sample of 244 were not reviewable because of incomplete documentation.
[4] The point estimate error rate for the sample is 5.91 percent with a precision of ± 2.52 percent.
[5] The point estimate number of error applications is 141 with a precision of ± 57 applications.

Appendix V

High-Level Organizational Chart
of Offices Referenced in This Report

The following is a high-level organizational chart of offices we discuss in this report, starting with the Deputy Commissioner for Services and Enforcement, who reports to the IRS Commissioner.

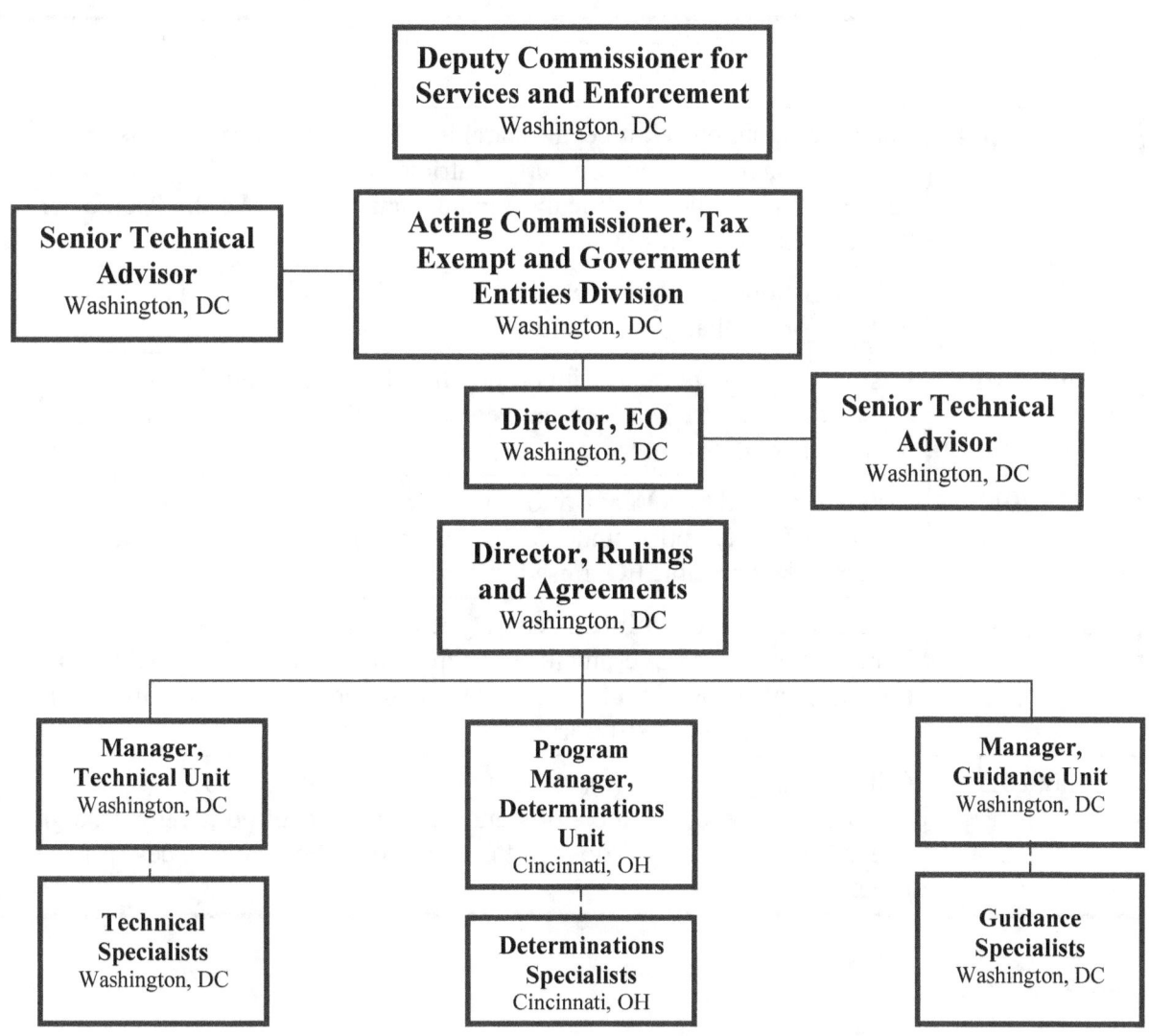

Appendix VI

Timeline of Written Criteria for Identifying Potential Political Cases

The following illustrates the changes to the written criteria provided to Determinations Unit employees for identifying applications for the team of specialists.

Date	Criteria Developed or Actions Taken
February 2010	****************************1***************************** ***************************1**************.
March–April 2010	The Determinations Unit began searching for other requests for tax exemption involving the Tea Party, Patriots, 9/12, and I.R.C. § 501(c)(4) applications involving political sounding names, *e.g.*, "We the People" or "Take Back the Country."
July 2010	Determinations Unit management requested its specialists to be on the lookout for Tea Party applications.
August 2010	First BOLO listing issued with criteria listed as "…various local organizations in the Tea Party movement…applying for exemption under 501(c)(3) or 501(c)(4)."
July 2011	Criteria changed to "Organizations involved with political, lobbying, or advocacy for exemption under 501(c)(3) or 501(c)(4)" based on the concerns the Director, EO, raised in June 2011.
January 2012	Criteria changed to "Political action type organizations involved in limiting/expanding government, educating on the constitution and bill of rights, social economic reform/movement" based on Determinations Unit concerns that the July 2011 criteria was too generic.
May 2012	Criteria changed to "501(c)(3), 501(c)(4), 501(c)(5), and 501(c)(6) organizations with indicators of significant amounts of political campaign intervention (raising questions as to exempt purpose and/or excess private benefit)."

Comprehensive Timeline of Events

The following chart illustrates a timeline of events from February 2010 through July 2012 involving the identification and processing of potential political cases. It shows that there was confusion about how to process the applications, delays in the processing of the applications, and a lack of management oversight and guidance. The timeline was developed using documentation provided by the EO function as well as numerous interviews with EO function personnel.

Date	Event	Additional Details	Source
February 25, 2010	*****************]***********************		E-Mail
Around March 1, 2010	The Determinations Unit Group Manager asked a specialist to search for other Tea Party or similar organizations' applications in order to determine the scope of the issue. The specialist continued to complete searches for additional cases until the precursor to the BOLO listing was issued in May 2010.	Determinations Unit personnel indicated that they used the description Tea Party as a shorthand way of referring to the group of cases involving political campaign intervention rather than to target any particular group. The specialist used Tea Party, Patriots, and 9/12 as part of the criteria for these searches.	Interview
March 16–17, 2010	Ten Tea Party cases were identified. The Acting Manager, Technical Unit, requested two more cases be transferred to Washington, D.C. ************************]********************	Not all of the ten cases had Tea Party in their names.	E-Mail
April 1–2, 2010	The new Acting Manager, Technical Unit, suggested the need for a Sensitive Case Report on the Tea Party cases. The Determinations Unit Program Manager agreed.		E-Mail
April 5, 2010	***************]***************************		E-Mail
April 5, 2010	A Determinations Unit specialist developed a list of 18 identified Tea Party cases during a search of applications. Three had already been approved as tax-exempt.	While the heading of the document listing these 18 cases referred to Tea Party cases, not all of the organizations listed had Tea Party in their names.	E-Mail

Date	Event	Additional Details	Source
April 19, 2010	The first Sensitive Case Report was prepared by the Technical Unit.	Sensitive Case Reports are shared with the Director, Rulings and Agreements, and a chart summarizing all Sensitive Case Reports is provided to the Director, EO.	Documentation
April 25–26, 2010	The Determinations Unit Program Manager requested Technical Unit contacts for the specialist assigned to work other Tea Party cases. Contacts were received. ***************************1***************** ********************		E-Mail
May 17, 2010	The Determinations Unit specialist will send additional information request letters to the Technical Unit for review prior to issuance as part of the Technical Unit's attempt to provide assistance to the Determinations Unit.		E-Mail
May 26, 2010	******************1************************ *************		E-Mail
May 27, 2010	The Technical Unit began reviewing additional information request letters prepared by the Determinations Unit.		Interview and E-Mail
June 7, 2010	Determinations Unit began training its specialists on emerging issues to watch for, including an emerging issue referred to as Tea Party Cases.		Documentation
June 14, 2010	******************1***********************		E-Mail
June 30, 2010	******************1***********************	**********1**********	E-Mail
July 2010	Determinations Unit management requested its specialists to be on the lookout for Tea Party applications.		E-Mail
July 2, 2010	******************1***********************		E-Mail
July 27, 2010	Prior to the BOLO listing development, an e-mail was sent updating the description of applications involving potential political campaign intervention and providing a coordinator contact for the cases. The description was changed to read, "These cases involve various local organizations in the Tea Party movement [that] are applying for exemption under 501(c)(3) or 501(c)(4)."		Interview and Documentation

Date	Event	Additional Details	Source
August 12, 2010	The BOLO listing was developed by the Determinations Unit in order to replace the existing practice of sending separate e-mails to all Determinations Unit employees as to cases to watch for, potentially abusive cases, cases requiring processing by the team of specialists, and emerging issues. The description of applications involving potential political campaign intervention on the BOLO listing was the same description used in the July 27, 2010, e-mail.		Interview and Documentation
August 2010	The responsibility for applications involving potential political campaign intervention was moved to a different team of specialists as part of a group realignment within the Determinations Unit.		Interview and Documentation
October 2010	Applications involving potential political campaign intervention were transferred to another Determinations Unit specialist. The specialist did not work on the cases while waiting for guidance from the Technical Unit.	Per the Director, Rulings and Agreements, there was a miscommunication about not working the cases while waiting for guidance.	Interviews
October 19, 2010	Technical Unit personnel forwarded a memorandum to their Acting Manager describing the work completed on the Tea Party cases by the Technical Unit. Included was a list of the cases the Technical Unit had assisted the Determinations Unit with.	The list included 40 cases, 18 of which did not have Tea Party in their names.	E-Mail
October 26, 2010	Determinations Unit personnel raised concerns to the Technical Unit with the approach being used to develop the Tea Party cases: Why does the Technical Unit need to review every additional information request letter when a template letter could be approved and used on all the cases?		E-Mail
November 16, 2010	A new coordinator contact for potential political cases was announced.		Interview and Documentation
November 16–17, 2010	A Determinations Unit Group Manager raised concern to the Determinations Unit Area Manager that they are still waiting for an additional information request letter template from the Technical Unit for the Tea Party cases. The coordinator had received calls from taxpayers checking on the status of their applications.		E-Mail
November 17, 2010	The Determinations Unit Program Manager discussed Tea Party cases with the Technical Unit manager. Review of the cases by the Technical Unit found that not all of the cases had the same issues so a template letter had not been developed.		E-Mail

Date	Event	Additional Details	Source
December 13, 2010	The Determinations Unit Program Manager asked the Technical Unit manager for a status on the Tea Party cases. The Technical Unit manager responded that they were going to discuss the cases with the Senior Technical Advisor to the Director, EO, shortly.		E-Mail
January 28, 2011	The Determinations Unit Program Manager requested an update on the Tea Party cases from the Technical Unit Acting Manager.		E-Mail
January 2011	A new person took over the Technical Unit Acting Manager role.		Interview
February 3, 2011	The Technical Unit Acting Manager provided an update to the Determinations Unit Program Manager on the cases being worked by the Technical Unit. Letters were being developed and would be reviewed shortly.		E-Mail
March 2, 2011	A Determinations Unit Group Manager reminded the Determinations Unit Program Manager to follow up with the Technical Unit on the status of the Tea Party cases.		E-Mail
March 30, 2011	******************1**********************.[1]		E-Mail
March 31, 2011	The Determinations Unit Program Manager stated that, while waiting for assistance from the Technical Unit, the Determinations Unit still needed to work Tea Party cases to the extent possible.	This contradicts the October 2010 decision not to work cases until assistance is received from the Technical Unit and supports the statement of the Director, Rulings and Agreements, that there was a miscommunication about not working the cases while awaiting assistance.	E-Mail
April 13, 2011	****************1**************************.		E-Mail
June 1–2, 2011	The Acting Director, Rulings and Agreements, requested criteria used to identify Tea Party cases from the Determinations Unit Program Manager. The Determinations Unit Program Manager requested criteria from a Determinations Unit Group Manager.		E-Mail

[1] The Taxpayer Advocate Service is an independent organization within the IRS that provides assistance to taxpayers whose tax problems have not been resolved through normal IRS channels. Taxpayer Advocate Service employees must, at times, rely on assistance from employees assigned to other IRS functions. To request assistance, the Taxpayer Advocate Service issues an Operations Assistance Request specifying the actions needed to help resolve the taxpayer's problem.

Date	Event	Additional Details	Source
June 2, 2011	A Determinations Unit Group Manager provided criteria for identifying potential Tea Party cases to the Determinations Unit Program Manager. Information was then forwarded to the Acting Director, Rulings and Agreements.	These criteria are very different than the BOLO listing criteria available at the time.	E-Mail
June 6, 2011	****************************1***************** *****************************		E-Mail
June 6, 2011	The Acting Director, Rulings and Agreements, commented that the criteria being used to identify Tea Party cases may have resulted in over-inclusion. ************************1********************** **		E-Mail
June 6, 2011	The Determinations Unit Program Manager mentioned that the Determinations Unit needed assistance from the Technical Unit to ensure consistency.		E-Mail
June 29, 2011	A briefing was held with the Director, EO. The briefing paper noted that the Determinations Unit sent cases that met any of the criteria below to a designated team of specialists to be worked: • "Tea Party," "Patriots," or "9/12 Project" is referenced in the case file. • Issues include Government spending, Government debt, or taxes. • Education of the public via advocacy/lobbying to "make America a better place to live." • Statements in the case file criticize how the country is being run. Over 100 applications were identified by this time. It was decided to develop a guide sheet for processing these cases.	The briefing paper for the Director, EO, was prepared by Tax Law Specialists in the Technical Unit and the Guidance Unit and was reviewed by the Acting Manager, Technical Unit. A Guidance Unit specialist was the primary author of the briefing paper. During the briefing, the Director, EO, raised concerns over the language of the BOLO listing criteria. The Director, EO, instructed that the criteria be immediately revised.	Documentation and E-Mail
July 5, 2011	A conference call was held with the Technical Unit; the Director, EO; and the Determinations Unit Program Manager. They developed new criteria for identifying cases. The Determinations Unit Program Manager made changes to the BOLO listing. The criteria were changed to "organizations involved with political, lobbying, or advocacy for exemption under 501(c)(3) or 501(c)(4)."		E-Mail

Date	Event	Additional Details	Source
July 5, 2011	The EO function Headquarters office would be putting a document together with recommended actions for identified cases.		E-Mail
July 23, 2011	The Technical Unit was assigned a new person to coordinate with the Determinations Unit.		E-Mail
July 24, 2011	Work commenced on the guide sheet when the Acting Manager, Technical Unit, asked tax law specialists to draft a list of things for Determinations Unit specialists to look for when working these cases.		E-Mail
August 4, 2011	Rulings and Agreements office personnel held a meeting with Chief Counsel so that everyone would have the latest information on the issue.		E-Mail
August 4, 2011	A Guidance Unit specialist asked if Counsel would review a check sheet prior to issuance to the Determinations Unit. The Acting Director, Rulings and Agreements, responded that Counsel would review it prior to issuance.		E-Mail
August 10, 2011	*********************]*********************** *********************		Documentation
September 15, 2011	The Determinations Unit Program Manager sent a list of all identified cases to the Acting Director, Rulings and Agreements, so that the Technical Unit could complete a limited "triage" of the cases using available information from the electronic case files. A Technical Unit specialist reviewed the list to determine if any cases could be closed on merit or closed with an adverse determination letter. This triage was considered a third screening.		E-Mail
September 21, 2011	The draft guide sheet was sent for review and comment to various EO function Headquarters office employees.		E-Mail
October 2011	A new person took over as the Acting Director, Rulings and Agreements.		Interview
October 24, 2011	A Technical Unit manager forwarded initial triage results to the Determinations Unit.		E-Mail
October 25, 2011	Based on the categories and terminology used in the triage results spreadsheet, the Determinations Unit Program Manager was unclear what the Determinations Unit should do with the triage results – close cases, develop further, *etc.* – and requested the status on the guidance from the Technical Unit.		E-Mail

Date	Event	Additional Details	Source
October 26, 2011	A Technical Unit specialist provided further explanation of the triage results in an e-mail to the Determinations Unit Program Manager.		E-Mail
October 30, 2011	The Determinations Unit Program Manager contacted the Acting Manager, Technical Unit, asking additional questions regarding the triage results and requesting a status update on the Technical Unit guidance. *******************1************************* *******************1*************************		E-Mail
November 3, 2011	An updated draft version of the guide sheet was sent to EO function employees for comment.		E-Mail
November 6, 2011	The Acting Manager, Technical Unit, had a Technical Unit specialist provide more details on the triage results, and informed the Determinations Unit Program Manager that the guidance was being reviewed prior to issuance.		E-Mail
November 6, 2011	The Acting Director, Rulings and Agreements, informed the Acting Manager, Technical Unit, and the Determinations Unit Program Manager that, based on feedback received, the guidance developed would not work in its present form – it was "too lawyerly" to be useful and needed the Determinations Unit input.		Interview and E-Mail
November 15, 2011	The Determinations Unit Program Manager forwarded the Technical Unit specialist's triage results to the Senior Technical Advisor to the Director, EO, per the Director's request.		E-Mail
November 22, 2011	The Acting Manager, Technical Unit, forwarded the clarified triage results to the Determinations Unit Program Manager.		E-Mail
November 23–30, 2011	A new Determinations Unit coordinator was assigned oversight of the cases by a Determinations Unit Group Manager. The draft Technical Unit guidance was provided to the Group Manager. The coordinator began working cases after receiving the guidance in anticipation of a team being assembled to work the cases.		Interview and E-Mail
November 2011	The Determinations Unit specialist assigned the cases began working them after receiving the draft Technical Unit guidance.		Interview

Date	Event	Additional Details	Source
December 7–9, 2011	A team of Determinations Unit specialists was created to review all the identified cases. An employee from Quality Assurance was also part of the team. The Technical Unit provided contacts for them.		E-Mail
December 16, 2011	The first meeting was held by the team of specialists.		Interview and E-Mail
January 2012	The first batch of letters requesting additional information for applications containing incomplete or missing information was issued by Determinations Unit specialists based, in part, on their reading of the draft guidance issued by the Technical Unit.		Interview and E-Mail
January 2012	A Determinations Unit specialist was tasked with performing a secondary screening of identified potential political cases to ensure that they involved political activities and not just general or lobbying advocacy.		Interviews
January 25, 2012	The BOLO listing criteria were again updated. The criteria was revised as "political action type organizations involved in limiting/expanding Government, educating on the Constitution and Bill of Rights, social economic reform/movement." The coordinator contact was changed as well.		Interview and Documentation
February 27, 2012	A member of the team of specialists asked when to start issuing additional information request letters to applicants again.		E-Mail
February 27, 2012	The Determinations Unit Program Manager questioned why the team of specialists was not issuing additional information request letters. The Determinations Unit Group Manager for the team of specialists had told the team coordinator to stop developing template questions, not to stop issuing additional information request letters. The miscommunication was corrected on February 29, 2012.		E-Mail
February 29, 2012	The Director, EO, requested that the Acting Director, Rulings and Agreements, develop a letter to clearly inform applicants what was going to happen if they did not respond to the additional information request letters and giving them more time for their responses.		E-Mail

Date	Event	Additional Details	Source
February 29, 2012	The Director, EO, stopped any more additional information request letters from being issued on advocacy cases until new guidance was provided to the Determinations Unit. In addition, the Acting Director, Rulings and Agreements, discussed with the Determinations Unit Program Manager about having specialists print out website information and asking the organizations to verify the information instead of asking for applicants to print out the website information.		E-Mail
February–March 2012	Numerous news articles began to be published with complaints from Tea Party organizations about the IRS's unfair treatment. Congress also began to show interest in the IRS's treatment of Tea Party organizations.		Documentation
March 2012	A new person became Acting Group Manager of the team of specialists.		Interview
March 1, 2012	A draft list of template questions was prepared by the team of specialists and forwarded to the Guidance Unit.	Questions included asking for donor information.	E-Mail
March 5, 2012	The Acting Manager, Technical Unit, established procedures for reviewing the first favorable determination letter drafted by the Determinations Unit.		E-Mail
March 6, 2012	***************1**************************** **********************		E-Mail
March 8, 2012	The Deputy Commissioner for Services and Enforcement requested that, if a taxpayer called about having to provide donor information, the Determinations Unit would allow them to not send the donor names but would inform them that the IRS may need it later.		E-Mail
March 8, 2012	The Acting Director, Rulings and Agreements, sent to the Determinations Unit Program Manager for comment a draft letter on giving applicants additional time to respond to the additional information request letters. The Determinations Unit Program Manager raised a concern of giving organizations that were not compliant with standard response timelines special treatment.		E-Mail
March 15, 2012	The Determinations Unit received guidance on how to handle different scenarios based upon the status of their cases. Those I.R.C. § 501(c)(4) organizations that had not responded to an additional information request letter were issued another letter giving them an additional 60 days to respond. Those letters were to be issued by March 16, 2012. This additional time letter was a one-time occurrence.		Interview and E-Mail

Date	Event	Additional Details	Source
March 23, 2012, and March 27, 2012	The Senior Technical Advisor to the Acting Commissioner, Tax Exempt and Government Entities Division, and the Deputy Commissioner for Services and Enforcement discussed concerns with the media attention the Tea Party applications were receiving. The Deputy Commissioner for Services and Enforcement asked the Senior Technical Advisor to look into what was going on in the Determinations Unit and make recommendations.		Interview
April 2012	The Acting Director, Rulings and Agreements, learned that the BOLO listing criteria had been changed on January 25, 2012, and informed the Director, EO.		Interview
April 4, 2012	The Determinations Unit received the extension letter for issuance to I.R.C. § 501(c)(3) organizations that had not responded to a previous additional information request letter.		E-Mail
April 17, 2012	Tax Exempt and Government Entities Division Headquarters office employees received the Technical Unit triage results and the draft guidance provided by the Technical Unit. Template questions developed by the team of specialists were also provided.		E-Mail
April 23, 2012	Senior Technical Advisor to the Acting Tax Exempt and Government Entities Division Commissioner visited the Determinations Unit in Cincinnati, Ohio, with a group of EO function employees, and reviewed about half of the identified cases.		Interview
April 24, 2012	The Acting Director, Rulings and Agreements, requested that the Senior Technical Advisor to the Director, EO, review all the additional information request letters issued and identify troubling questions, which organizations received them, and which members of the team of specialists asked them.		E-Mail
April 25, 2012	The Senior Technical Advisor to the Director, EO, provided results of the additional information request letter review, including a list of troubling questions.	The results included the names of donors as a troubling question.	E-Mail
April 25, 2012	Chief Counsel's office provided additional comments on the draft guidance developed for the Determinations Unit.		E-Mail

Date	Event	Additional Details	Source
May 8, 2012	The Determinations Unit Program Manager was informed that EO function Headquarters office employees planned to visit Cincinnati, Ohio, to provide training on cases and perform a review of the cases to recommend what additional actions, if any, were needed to make a determination.		E-Mail
May 9, 2012	The Director, Rulings and Agreements, asked about the process for updating the BOLO listing.		E-Mail
May 14–15, 2012	Training was held in Cincinnati, Ohio, on how to process identified potential political cases. The Senior Technical Advisor to the Director, EO, took over coordination of the team of specialists from the Determinations Unit.		E-Mail
May 16, 2012	A joint team of Determinations Unit specialists and EO function Headquarters office employees began reviewing all potential political cases began in Cincinnati, Ohio. Cases were divided into four groups with recommendations for how to proceed: favorable determination, favorable with limited development, significant development, and probably adverse. This took around three weeks to complete. A worksheet was used to document the reviews.		E-Mail
May 17, 2012	The Director, Rulings and Agreements, issued a memorandum outlining new procedures for updating the BOLO listing. The BOLO listing criteria were updated again. New criteria reads: "501(c)(3), 501(c)(4), 501(c)(5), and 501(c)(6) organizations with indicators of significant amounts of political campaign intervention (raising questions as to exempt purpose and/or excess private benefit)."	Suggested additions and changes must be approved by a Determinations Unit coordinator, the Determinations Unit Program Manager, and the Director, Rulings and Agreements.	Interview and E-Mail
May 21, 2012	The EO function determined that the requested donor information could be destroyed or returned to the applicant if not used to make the final determination of tax-exempt status. It does not need to be kept in the administrative file. A letter would be issued to the organizations informing them that the donor information was destroyed.		Interview and E-Mail
May 24, 2012	A telephone call script was developed to inform some organizations that had not responded to the additional information requests that it was not necessary to send the requested information and that their applications had been approved. Also, an additional paragraph was developed for the determination letter.		E-Mail

Date	Event	Additional Details	Source
May 2012	After the review of identified cases was completed, each Determinations Unit specialist working cases was assigned a Technical Unit employee to work with on the cases. The Technical Unit employee reviewed all additional information request letters prior to issuance. The Quality Assurance Unit began reviewing 100 percent of the cases prior to closure. The Quality Assurance Unit review will shift from 100 percent review to a sample review once a comfort level with the results of the quality review was achieved.		Interview
May 2012	A decision was made to refer cases to the Review of Operations Unit for follow-up if there were indications of political campaign intervention but not enough to prevent approval of tax-exempt status.		Interview and E-Mail
June 4, 2012	A draft letter was developed to send to organizations that provided donor information. The letter would inform the organizations that the information was destroyed.		E-Mail
June 7, 2012	The Director, Rulings and Agreements, provided guidance on how to process cases now that they had been reviewed and divided into categories. Any new cases received would go through the same review process prior to assignment.		E-Mail
July 15, 2012	A new Acting Determinations Unit Group Manager was overseeing the team of specialists.		Interview

Appendix VIII

Management's Response to the Draft Report

COMMISSIONER
TAX EXEMPT AND
GOVERNMENT ENTITIES
DIVISION

DEPARTMENT OF THE TREASURY
INTERNAL REVENUE SERVICE
WASHINGTON, D.C. 20224

APR 3 0 2013

MEMORANDUM FOR DEPUTY INSPECTOR GENERAL FOR AUDIT

FROM: Joseph H. Grant, Acting Commissioner, Tax Exempt and
           Government Entities

SUBJECT: "Inappropriate Criteria Were Used to Identify Tax-Exempt
           Applications for Review"

Thank you for the opportunity to review the draft report and for your review of this issue. We appreciate your recommendations for improvements to our processes.

We recognize that some errors occurred in the handling of the influx of advocacy cases and we appreciate TIGTA's acknowledgment of our steps to improve the process. As further outlined below, significant improvements in this area are in place and we are confident that what transpired here will not recur.

We believe it is important to put this matter into context. Starting in 2010, Exempt Organizations (EO) observed a significant increase in the number of section 501(c)(3) and section 501(c)(4) applications from organizations that appeared to be, or planned to be, engaged in political campaign activity. Between 2008 and 2012, the number of applications for section 501(c)(4) status more than doubled. We also received numerous referrals from the public, media, watchdog groups, and members of Congress alleging that specific section 501(c)(4) organizations were engaged in political campaign activity to an impermissible extent.

Similar to our approach in other areas (e.g., credit counseling, down payment assistance organizations, etc.), EO sought to assign cases to designated employees. Centralization of like cases ensures that specific employees who have been trained on the relevant issues can adequately review the applications. In this way the IRS learns of new trends (as was the case in credit counseling), and can approach cases in a uniform way to promote consistency and quality. While this is the correct approach for handling certain classes of cases, centralization does slow the progress of some applications (at least initially). Therefore, it is important to take this action only in appropriate situations and to designate cases for centralization in an equitable manner.

It is our view that centralization was warranted in this situation. First, it is important to recognize the intensely fact-specific nature of the determination of whether an organization is described in section 501(c)(4). To be recognized as exempt under section 501(c)(4), an organization must be engaged primarily in the promotion of social welfare. This requires a review of all activities, a classification of activities into those that promote social welfare and those that do not, and a balancing of both classes of activities. Note that the promotion of social welfare does not include political campaign intervention. And in cases where there is the potential of political campaign intervention, the application process becomes even more difficult. EO must first determine whether any activities described in the application constitute political campaign intervention and must also determine whether the applicant is primarily engaged in social welfare activity in light of any political campaign intervention and any other non-exempt activity. There are no bright line tests for what constitutes political campaign intervention (in particular, the line between such activity and education) or whether an organization is primarily engaged in social welfare activities.

The second reason that centralization was warranted in this case is that the applications EO began to receive in 2010 were in many cases vague as to the activities the applicants planned to conduct. Many applications included what appeared to be incomplete or inconsistent information. For example, a number of applications indicated that the organization did not plan to conduct political campaign activity, but elsewhere described activities that appeared in fact to be such activity. It was also clear that many organizations did not understand what activities would constitute political campaign intervention under the tax law. For these reasons, it was necessary in many cases for us to gather additional information. And we believe it was important that we be consistent in how we developed these cases.

While centralization was warranted, the manner in which we initially designated cases for centralization was inappropriate. We should centralize like cases by a review of the facts contained in the application and not just by name. While it is necessary to consider a variety of information in the screening process (including flags for current emerging issues) we recognize that selection based on organization name was not appropriate for these cases. As the report discusses, we have a new approval process by which we designate a class of cases for centralization. Decisions with respect to the centralized collection of cases must be made at a much higher level of the organization. We believe this will prevent a recurrence of what happened in this case.

The report also describes mistakes that were made in the process by which these applications were worked. The IRS recognizes that there were delays and, in some instances, information requests that were overbroad. As the report notes, we took steps to modify the original approach. First, we reviewed all cases to determine the appropriate scope of review for each case. We also established a process by which each assigned revenue agent works in coordination with a specific technical expert. With respect to information requests, in some cases the Internal Revenue Manual prescribed deadlines for applicants to respond were too short, and we requested donor names unnecessarily. In these instances, we informed organizations that they had more time and that we would work with them if they could provide the

2

information we requested in an alternative manner. In cases in which the donor names were not used in making the determination, the donor information was expunged from the file.

It is important to understand that centralization of these cases did not dictate how the case ultimately was or will be resolved. As the report illustrates, EO's selection of an organization for further development does not mean that EO will deny the application, but means that EO needs to resolve questions arising from the application before we can grant tax-exemption. Moreover, the majority of cases selected for full development were not selected based on the organizations' names. Finally, all cases, whether selected by name or not, were worked in the same fashion.

The results to date support our approach. Of the nearly 300 section 501(c)(4) advocacy cases, to date we have approved more than 120 (nearly 30 have withdrawn their requests). Note that the report appears to view approvals as evidence that EO should not have looked closely at those applications. That is not the case. Many of these organizations did not supply enough information in their initial applications to merit approval so that further development was necessary. In many cases, this further development and back-and-forth discussion with the taxpayer allowed EO to conclude that the legal requirements were satisfied and allowed the applicant to better understand its responsibilities and the law.

EO is dedicated to reviewing applications for tax-exempt status in an impartial manner. Centralization of like cases furthers quality and consistency. The mistakes outlined in the report resulted from the lack of a set process for working the increase in advocacy cases and insufficient sensitivity to the implications of some of the decisions made. We believe the front line career employees that made the decisions acted out of a desire for efficiency and not out of any political or partisan viewpoint. And as the report discusses, these issues have been resolved.

Our response to your recommendations is found in the attachment. If you have any questions about this response, please contact Lois G. Lerner, Director, Exempt Organizations, at 202-283-8848.

Attachment

3

Attachment

Recommendation 1: Ensure that the memorandum requiring the Director, Rulings and Agreements, to approve all original entries and changes to criteria included on the BOLO listing prior to implementation be formalized in the appropriate Internal Revenue Manual.

Corrective Action: We will ensure that the procedures set forth in the memorandum requiring the Director, Rulings and Agreements, to approve in advance all original entries and changes to the BOLO are made part of the Internal Revenue Manual.

Implementation Date: September 30, 2013

Responsible Official: Director, Exempt Organizations

Recommendation 2: Develop procedures to better document the reason(s) applications are chosen for review by the team of specialists (e.g., evidence of specific political campaign intervention in the application file or specific reasons the EO function may have for choosing to review the application further based on past experience).

Corrective Action: We will review our screening procedures to determine whether, and to what extent, additional documentation can be implemented without having an adverse impact on the timeliness of our case processing.

Implementation Date: September 30, 2013

Responsible Official: Director, Exempt Organizations

(Note: We consolidate here the text of Recommendations 3, 5, 6 and 9, and we provide a single, consolidated response to these recommendations following the text of Recommendation 9, below.)

Recommendation 3: Develop training or workshops to be held before each election cycle including, but not limited to, the proper ways to identify applications that require review of political campaign intervention activities.

Recommendation 5: Develop guidance for specialists on how to process requests for tax-exempt status involving potentially significant political campaign intervention. This guidance should also be posted to the Internet to provide transparency to organizations on the application process.

1

Recommendation 6: Develop training or workshops to be held before each election cycle including, but not limited to: a) what constitutes political campaign intervention versus general advocacy (including case examples) and b) the ability to refer for follow-up those organizations that may conduct activities in a future year which may cause them to lose their tax-exempt status.

Recommendation 9: The Director, EO, should develop training or workshops to be held before each election cycle including, but not limited to, how to word questions in additional information request letters and what additional information should be requested.

Corrective Action: We will develop training on the topics described in the recommendations 3, 5, 6, and 9. Because election cycles are continuous, we will develop a schedule that ensures staff have the training as needed to handle potential political intervention matters.

Implementation Date: January 31, 2014

Responsible Official: Director, Exempt Organizations

Recommendation 4: Develop a process for the Determinations Unit to formally request assistance from the Technical Unit and the Guidance Unit. The process should include actions to initiate, track, and monitor requests for assistance to ensure that requests are responded to timely.

Corrective Action: We will develop a formal process for Determinations to request assistance and to monitor such requests.

Implementation Date: June 30, 2013

Responsible Official: Director, Exempt Organizations

Recommendation 7: Provide oversight to ensure that potential political cases, some of which have been in process for three years, are approved or denied expeditiously.

Corrective Action: While this is an ongoing project, we are closely overseeing the remaining open cases to ensure that we reach determinations as expeditiously as possible.

Implementation Date: April 30, 2013

Responsible Official: Director, Exempt Organizations

2

Recommendation 8: Recommend to IRS Chief Counsel and the Department of the Treasury that guidance on how to measure the "primary activity" of I.R.C. § 501(c)(4) social welfare organizations be included for consideration in the Department of the Treasury Priority Guidance Plan.

Corrective Action: We will share this recommendation with the IRS Chief Counsel and Treasury Office of Tax Policy.

Implementation Date: May 3, 2013

Responsible Official: Acting Commissioner, Tax Exempt and Government Entities

3

www.ingramcontent.com/pod-product-compliance
Lightning Source LLC
Chambersburg PA
CBHW081903170526
45167CB00007B/3135